What I Wish for You

To _____

From _____

What I Wish for You

WRITTEN BY
Isaac David Garuda

COVER ART AND ILLUSTRATIONS BY
Alexandra Hardy-Shamaya

Hardy-Shamaya Publishing
Tucson, Arizona

Cover and artwork by
Alexandra Hardy-Shamaya

The cover is a copy of an original 4' X 6' acrylic painting entitled "garden of the Heart." It is a love story on canvas. A limited edition, signed lithograph, 18-2/3' X 28", is available for purchase from the Publisher for $100.00 (price subject to change).

See website for book and more artwork: www.shamaya.com

Published by
Hardy-Shamaya Publishing
P. O. Box 64783
Tucson, Arizona 85718

Introduction

This is a book born of love. It communicates heartfelt wishes encouraging the reader to live a full, healthy, vibrant life. Its simple, straight-forward messages reach deep into the core of our humanity and touch us in ways that we know are true.

What I Wish for You will call you to live the kind of life you want for yourself and for those you love. It is a book to be read over and over again, and a book to be given to friends and family. Read it, enjoy it, and take its messages to heart, for you deserve everything that is wished for you in the following pages.

1

Inspiration
Nurturance
Patience
Integrity
Sanctuary
Vitality
Desire
Innocence
Self-Acceptance

Inspiration

May you dream magnificent dreams
and awaken
to make them come true.

Nurturance

M ay you consistently make time
to do those things that remind you
it's great to be you.

Patience

`May you always remember
that the course of human events
rarely goes according to one's
personal timetable.

May your sense of self-worth
protect you from ever pretending
to be someone or something you are not.

Sanctuary

`May your home always be a place
of warmth,
caring,
friendship and sharing.

Vitality

$\grave{\text{M}}$ay you find
plenty of physical energy
for playing the game of life to its fullest.

Desire

May you be blessed with strong intentions
about
those things in life
you endeavor to undertake and accomplish.

Innocence

May you love the child in you
that is playful, inquisitive, sparkling, blameless,
and full of wonder.

Self-Acceptance

May you accept your errors and transmute them
from the bitterness of self-blame
to the sweetness of self-love.

II

Friendship
Self-Expression
Direction
Depth
Self-Possession
Balance
Reverence
Courage

Friendship

May you have many wonderful friends who love you
just the way you are,
yet challenge you to be
all that you can be.

Self-Expression

May you laugh heartily, cry openly,
sing loudly,
dance wildly,
love unashamedly.

Direction

May you discover
    the true purpose of your existence
and pursue that purpose
        with vigor, grace, and a very good sense of humor.

Depth

May your life be filled with
people,
places, and
things
that touch you at the core of your being.

Self-Possession

May you appreciate your own company
and enjoy times
of quiet and solitude.

Balance

May you bring a sense of
playfulness
as well as
practicality to all your endeavors.

Reverence

May you value, honor and esteem
your- and every other self
as sacred units
of the one Unity.

Courage

May you stand steady
in the face of the one aspect of life that is certain;
namely uncertainty.

III

Trust
Intelligence
Work
Spice
Confidence
Presence
Passion
Well-Being
Wisdom

Trust

May you not burden yourself
with a need to make sense
out of everything.

Intelligence

May you see the futility of placing blame,
finding fault,
or making excuses
in relation to what you experience.

Work

May you find creative work
that nourishes your spirit with joy
and fills your pocketbook with green.

Spice

May you lead a vivid life,
richly textured with many glorious
sights   sounds   smells   tastes   touches.

Confidence

May you follow the dictates of your heart,
regardless
of what other people may think of you.

Presence

NOW

May you abide in the ever-changing Now,
knowing that nothing is real
but a present moment.

Passion

May you touch the lives
of all who meet you
by the very force of your spirit and love.

Well-Being

May you honor the needs of the body and spirit
so as to experience good health
always.

Wisdom

May you let
your intuitive self become
the supreme authority in your life, and
may you always trust what you know from that self.

IV

Perseverence
Humor
Healing
Objectivity
Heart
Breath
Freedom
Abundance

Perseverence

May you welcome obstacles
as opportunities to express yourself
in ways you didn't think possible.

Humor

May you cultivate the ability to laugh at yourself
and
eliminate the habit of feeling sorry for yourself.

Healing

May you allow
the unresolved hurts, frustrations, and fears from the past
to seek their release in the present
and thus be healed once and for all time.

Objectivity

May you give yourself permission
to experience and express
everything you feel as a person,
without taking anything personally.

Heart

May you feel a deep sense of compassion
for yourself and others
at those times
when life is difficult.

Breath

May you feel so at home in your body
that you always breathe
deeply,
easily, and
freely.

Freedom

May you live each moment free
of worry about the future
and regret about the past.

Abundance

May you tap the spiritual riches within you,
from which flows
everything you need to live the exact life
your heart desires.

V

Recognition
Romance
Responsibility
Spirituality
Vision
Excitement
Mastery
Joy

Recognition

May you realize
what an incredible Being
you are.

Romance

May you join with a mate
and together share
as much love and affection
as anyone could ever want.

Responsibility

May you know yourself as the generator
of your inner feelings
as well as your overt actions.

Spirituality

May you be moved
in the direction of an oceanic experience
of the perfection and Unity
in all things.

Vision

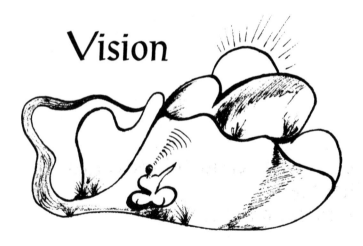

May you see and appreciate things as they are
rather than
as they seem to be.

Excitement

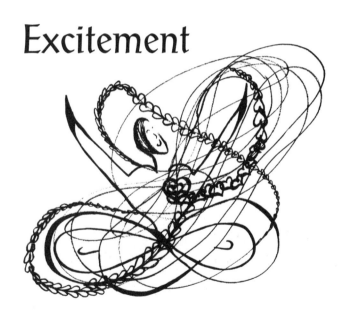

May your life be a stirring ride
through the mysteries of consciousness
and the wonders of the world.

Mastery

May you realize
        a wondrous, fulfilling life
            that serves one paramount purpose;
the good of all that is.

Joy

And last,
   but not least,
may you live with outrageous joyfulness
            in all your years.

Postscript

In January 1993, author Isaac David Garuda, was considering how to honor his son Matthew's upcoming 22nd birthday when he had what he calls "a heart inspiration." A succession of warm, loving wishes suddenly flooded his awareness and he wrote them to Matthew in the form of a letter.

The act of writing these wishes down on paper moved Isaac deeply. He showed his letter to a few close friends before mailing it and they too were touched. Their strong responses convinced Isaac and Alexandra Hardy-Shamaya to publish what he'd written in a little gift book of wishes with universal meaning. Thus *What I Wish for You* came into being.

If Isaac's book, born out of love for his son, has touched your heart also, perhaps you will want to give it as a gift to your friends and loved ones. Additional copies can be purchased by sending a check or money order for $12.00 (postage and handling included) per book to:

Hardy-Shamaya Publishing
P. O. Box 64783
Tucson, Arizona 85718

Isaac would be delighted to learn of your response to his book and he invites you to write to him at the above address.

Acknowledgments

Many wonderful people have contributed to the publication of this book. Among them are the following:

Kendall Morse, my friend and wordsmith of the highest order, for editing the original manuscript and turning it into a literary piece worth publishing.

John Davis and Arizona Lithographers, who believed in the book and gave of their expertise to enable its publication.

Diana Hunter, book packager, who shepherded this project over hill and dale with sensitivity and creative energy.

Penny Smith, typographer extraordinaire, whose company, TypeWorks, did a masterful job of putting the words and illustrations together.

Laurel Gregory, whose friendship and encouragement launched this project out of the idea stage into a reality.

Alexandra Hardy-Shamaya, whose incredible artwork brings so much aliveness to this book and to the world.

And finally, my first-born son, Matthew Jacob Fischer, whose presence in my life gave birth to *What I Wish for You.*

Thank you one and all from the bottom of my heart.

I.D.G.